John's Virtual School Journey

John Xavier

Written By: John Xavier

© 2020

ALL RIGHTS RESERVED. No part of this book may be reproduced in any written, electronic, recording, or photocopying without written permission of the publisher or author. The exception would be in the case of brief quotations embodied in the critical articles or reviews and pages where permission is specifically granted by the publisher or author.

Publishing Service By: Pen Legacy®

Formatting By: Junnita Jackson

Cover By: Alexis Robinson

Library of Congress Cataloging – in- Publication Data has been applied for.

Paperback ISBN: 9781735879864

PRINTED IN THE UNITED STATES OF AMERICA.

John likes school. He likes reading books in the library.

He also likes playing kickball with his friends.

John's favorite subject at school is science. He loves doing experiments like making volcanoes out of clay and mixing ingredients to see the reaction.

Today is a special day for John because he finds out what he will learn this school year in Ms. Jeri's class.

"I can't wait for the school year to start!" John beams. "Mrs. Jeri said we would have spiders as are class pets this year!"

"John, sweetie," his mom sighs. "This year is going to be a little different. You will have to learn from home."

He was looking forward to seeing his friends and being back in Ms. Jeri's class.
"But why?" John cries. "I want to see my friends! I don't want to be all alone!"
"It won't be so bad," John's mom says with a small smile. "What if you think of it as an experiment?"

This idea makes John a little happy.

"Like a scientist?" He asks excitedly.

"Yup. Maybe you can build your own science lab. Each school day will be research for the new way of learning," his mom explains.

Now John has the perfect idea! "Let's go, Ruffles!" John says, turning to his dog. "We've got building to do!"

John races upstairs to his bedroom and starts planning his science lab.

"I'll need a desk, a lamp, and a thinker's chair," John says.

There's a knock at John's door. "Care to use some help with the research center?" Asks John's dad.

Together, John and his dad set up his brand new desk.

John draws pictures of spaceships and volcanoes. He even lets Ruffles add a special picture – his paw print.

Once the hard work is done, John is proud of his new classroom at home. "My classroom", John coughs to clear his throat, "I mean science lab is an awesome virtual learning space – I love it!" he shouts.

Today is John's first day of virtual school. John makes sure to wear his lab coat and favorite shirt to see all his classmates and Ms. Jeri online.

The classroom is full of familiar faces. Everyone is smiling and happy to see one another.

Ms. Jeri greets everyone with a huge smile, "Hello class! Welcome to our virtual classroom!"

"Wow, is that John? That's such a cool lab coat!" Ms. Jeri says as she gives John a thumbs up. Soon, John's classmates also compliment him on his lab coat and desk. "Thank you friends.

This year is our special research mission! We are discovering a new way to learn." says John.

"That's right, John," Ms. Jeri says.

"It's also time to recite our class motto:

I am smart. I can learn. I will study hard so I can earn, more Experience and knowledge galore. As my love for science, technology, and math soar, soar, soar...

Before John knows it, he has finished each lesson for his first day, and it's time to wave goodbye to Ms. Jeri and his classmates.

"I'll see everyone tomorrow for the next day of research!" John says with a big smile.

After closing his laptop, John goes downstairs to see his mom.

John runs into the kitchen to show his mom his drawing of a dinosaur climbing a volcano. "Oh, that's such a beautiful picture. How was your first day of school" his mom asks.

"It was fun! We went over math, colored pictures and read a cool book about outer space," John exclaims. "I also got to lead the class motto today."

John was so proud of his first day that he couldn't stop smiling.

"See? Virtual school isn't so bad," John's mom says. "Sometimes we have to find new ways to learn when the unexpected happens."

"Sounds a lot like science to me," John chuckles.

John's mom pulls him in close for a tight hug. "You're the best scientist I know, John. Now, how about a snack for all the hard research?"

14

Want to go on another journey? Get a copy of John Xavier's best-seller - John's Journey to Outer Space!

Astronauts and space are perennial kid-favorites. John's Journey to Outer Space offers an exciting look into the imagination of a young child who experiences many extraordinary galactic adventures in outer space. Written in an accessible and fun style, this imaginative text is perfectly complemented by visually stunning, large-sized, full-color illustrations.

This is the perfect book to encourage early learners to engage in science by using their imagination, thinking creatively and learning about basic cosmic terminology.

For more information about John Xavier visit JohnXCrew.com.

Printed in the USA
CPSIA information can be obtained
at www.ICGtesting.com
JSHW040902041223
52893JS00008B/70